waking at the bottom of the dark

JAN CLAUSEN

LONG HAUL PRESS

Long Haul Press, P.O. Box 592, Van Brunt Station, Brooklyn, N.Y. 11215

Some of these poems first appeared in: *Amazon Quarterly; Calyx; Cameos: New Small Press Women Poets* (Edited by Felice Newman; Crossing Press, 1978); *Conditions; Cottonwood Review; Feminist Studies; Greenfield Review; Heresies; Sailing the Road Clear; Sunbury.*

Copyright © 1979 by Jan Clausen. All rights reserved. No part of this book may be copied, reproduced, or used in any way without written permission from the author.

First edition, first printing.

Library of Congress Catalog Card Number 78-71983

ISBN 0-9602284-0-3

Cover design by Virginia Tan.

Typesetting by Jan Clausen.

for Elly

CONTENTS

THE STAKES

waking at the bottom of the dark	9
the empress anastasia in new york	10
i know a woman	16
a suicide	17
struggle	18
for a friend who finds my political commitment "tenuous" and wishes further clarification	21
invocation	22
pacific	23
ode: summer	24

WOMAN'S WORK/I

grandma	27
Sestina, Winchell's Donut House	28
tantrum	30
children	31
stories	37
the kitchen window	39

WOMAN'S WORK/II

likeness	47
the transplant	48
september again	49
december: two views	50
words for this	52
impermanence	57
the trees: connecticut	58

FLYING OVER MY LIFE

dialectics	63
flying over my life	71

*I don't mind bein' in jail
but I got to stay there so long.*

    —Bessie Smith, "Jail House Blues"

*And this is the moment we thought to be born
And, having measured time flawlessly,
So as not to miss any of the unprecedented
Spectacles, we took leave of non-being.*

    —Anna Akhmatova, "Prehistory"
      Translated by Rima Shore

*There is no escape. There is no turning
back.*

*To move is to be touched. To be flung, lucid,
against the inner layers of the rain.*

To know is to touch. To be killed by the sun.

    —Susan Sherman, "Areas of Silence"

THE STAKES

waking at the bottom of the dark

waking
at the bottom of the dark
to the love of your body
to drink cold tea
and stuff clothes in a sack
and help the sleepy child
with her difficult socks
i think of wartime
an evacuation

but you're only off
for a weekend in the country
and it is good
to be out walking early
a day so cold like this
dawn striped with clouds

although i suppose
the park is dangerous
there are old men walking dogs
there are thin young men
hunched down in their thin jackets
i am the only woman

yes i am the woman
whom personal happiness wraps
a magic coat
the windows are glazed with light
the trees shake out
their final green and gold
above the leaf-thick grass
the meadow opens, spacious
as a prairie

oh how can i remember:

*it was winter. clear. the light
was shining through the crystal
park.*

the empress anastasia in new york

> *Anastasia was long rumored to be the only member of the Tsar's immediate family to have escaped execution by the Bolsheviks.*

1.

it has begun
the rain

the rain-
shaped sleep
of women
who nod in doorways

dreaming of good times
bars and indian
summer

2.

in the dream
picture it is
august i am
standing on the grass
beside blue water
i am sixteen
full of zen and
existentialism
acid lust wearing
a two piece
bathing suit i
had my body then
browned, frowning
bored as havana
before the revolution

3.

in my mother's house there are
shelves well stocked with
cans, mixes, paper products.
dreams of land. dreams
of flight to the country.
these white-skinned dreams
of cities without color,
catastrophes we do not name.
these dreams of dreamless sleep,
remembering nothing

4.

she hid joints of mutton
beneath her skirt
her pockets bulged
pounds of butter
whole hams in her suit-
case the good bitter
taste of real coffee
in her mouth she roamed
streets freely
the soldiers never
caught her the jews
trooped off to treblinka

5.

in vietnam arthritis
is common due to
months years spent crouched
in damp bomb shelters

and i remember my
mother's soft
face skin with the
fallout scare
shelter with the
shelves lined with
canned peaches
jugs of water
the nuclear family
in the atomic age and
SAC is in the air

the bay of pigs cuban
missile crisis got
stuck in my childhood
throat my mother
moved the iron
back and forth she
listened about suez
on the radio

and mother still writes how she
hopes, keeps her shelves
stocked, how she helps
these expatriate vietnamese
who can't find jobs
in their adopted country

6.

please give me a little piece
of meat for
i cannot eat your bread
your unhulled rice

for i am a princess
in my own right
country

my grandmother's face
was famous
in the nineties

(and castro hid
in the mountains
the jungles covered
ho chi minh
and mao is whispered
change from out of the north
and lenin rode east
in a sealed train
and *iskra* means
a single spark
can start a prairie fire)

and we came
unto neon
dollar signed
miami

7.

the years
her mother singing
in her hair

you are the rightful
empress
anastasia

but she wakes in nightmare
screaming this word
"pretender"

mother
what really happened
in that cellar

8.

the streets get colder.
she grows more weary
of lies, potatoes,
her mother still
mourning the tsar.

her room looks out
on an airshaft. the carpet
is worn. the bronx
is burning. she never saw
the neva.

she pawns the last
of the icons.

9.

in spring she crosses
over, joins
the resistance

10.

this november
city is up
tight. in midtown
the ibm selectrics
have been bolted
to the desks
of secretaries
who are afraid, now
to change jobs.
the druggists refuse
to fill medicaid
prescriptions.
a man has been shot
for going
over the turnstiles.

we slept overnight
on long island,
all the way out.
i saw each grain
of sand a different
color, stuffed shells
in my coat. i walked
as before toward rain
down a beach shining
white through the storm,
watched the tide
turn once.

locked into the city,
i plan to quit my job.
i must get a jacket
with a working
zipper, call
the exterminator,
have a gate installed
on the fire escape
access window.

Thanksgiving, 1975

i know a woman

*thinking of the Symbionese Liberation Army,
and others*

i know a woman who takes a gun to bed
and, strange, it makes me proud to know she can.
the world is safe only when we are dead.

what would you give of everything you had?
what single act could rectify your sin?
i know a woman who takes a gun to bed.

cast off cold sleep, you cry; here's fire instead;
the heart unlocks; our pain is lit to the end;
the world is safe only when we are dead.

with thieves you weave your fate; outside, the crowd
that guts its lambs is ravenous to begin.
i know a woman who takes a gun to bed.

we buy the papers, read what the terrorists did.
we all agree they're quite insane; to them
the world is safe only when we are dead.

sisters, why do you lodge here in my head?
i am not hunted. nor am i to blame.
i know a woman who takes a gun to bed.
the world is safe only when we are dead.

a suicide

you are walking
to the rev-
olution, but you
aren't there
yet, aren't there
yet. always
the road stretches
out before
you, promising
an end, final
as death, to guilt.
you would cut
off a leg, you
think, if the pain
of others, broad-
cast live and
amplified inside
your head, would
stop. you cannot
stop yourself. you
run, staggering
now, through
freezing rain, and
you're not there
yet, not there
yet and it's
your fault. tired
to death, you
fall down in
the dark. self-
hatred rams you like
a ten ton truck.
come morning, you
lie there cold and
still yourself,
and the earth
turns, telling over
her ancient hurt.

struggle

1.

do friends
really end it over
politics?

how improbable it seems
sitting out in the soft air
on the warm steps
in mid-Manhattan
vapid with pastels,
with April

well, it has been coming
on for months, for years

positions
have hardened

2.

you are giving her up
she has given up contradictions

it will be awkward
at all the demonstrations

3.

except for (years ago)
one miserable half-night
you were never lovers

the inconvenience
should be minimal

no furniture
no bank account
no lease
no custody of cats
to be arranged

there's just
your investment
in history/her face
elongated in the wide-
brimmed hat, not wanting
to be told she
looked like ruling-
class V. Woolf, but
laughing at it

4.

she knows/you don't know
what will make
this revolution

*it's about the most
combative forces
it's about struggle*

it's all about doctrine
and you don't go to church

the holy martyrs
looked like this
at the stake
manic
seeing only the one
thing

*is confronting white
supremacy arrogant?
the contradiction
is not antagonistic*

*i believe in political
struggle among friends*

yes, but you're tired

5.

now you will put her
in her place with words:

*lapsed Catholic
ultra-left sectarian*

now you will struggle
only in the dreams
in which, herself
and casual, she phones;
herself and more,
and hardly casual
against a backdrop
of South Bronx or jail
she lets you in
on her dangerous
simple life:
sets the explosive
lights the cigarette
screams when the torture warrants
shoots to kill

but words cannot reduce her
to a word

dreams
cannot reduce her to a dream

what if she is wrong?
what if she is right?

*it was the last time
i saw her
alive*

for a friend who finds my political commitment "tenuous" and wishes further clarification

yes, "tenuous"
delicate and frail
as the human chance itself in this century

about this thing
i refuse anymore to lie

now you must take me as i
stand
stripped
my own witness

no, i have
nothing to offer

but what i really think
what i really see

who, changing, but
always myself
i am

invocation

glass sequins
the park paths.

november's leaves
blow back

like another fall.
kids huddle

on nineteenth century steps,
smoke grass.

march wind, raw
as a sore throat,

strip the sleep
from my eyes.

uncover my sadness.
lift me. let me look.

pacific

ocean

you blue
calm mother

heal me

like a good
army surgeon

send me
back to brooklyn

ode: summer

and sulfur oxides
still corrode our lungs
particulate matter
fuzzes the jersey shore
pregnant women
faint at unemployment
street-schooled children
play at being free
those who can pay
have gone to amagansett
a neighbor screams *faggot*
into the telephone
the static carries
the politicians talk
we remember our bodies
and sleep in a sweat
of buildings, knowing
the stakes

WOMAN'S WORK/ I

grandma

for fifty years
his breathing at my back
then separate rooms
and then his blindness
terror of the dark
then even that light gone

i visit his body
in the nursing home
i clean this house
and hope for another summer
a few tomatoes

the amputation
arrives almost too late

my children come
heavy with money
and middle age
complaining of daughters
who refuse to marry

but more and more
i want to be alone

sometimes i remember
a winter i taught school
in a border district
it was before the war

there were nights i walked
the path, the icebound river
miles from the nearest farm
unafraid, wolves howling
on the frozen shore

Sestina, Winchell's Donut House

Watching the black hours through to morning
I'd set out each successive tray of grease-
cooked donuts on the rack, chocolate and pink-
frosted, to harden beneath the fluorescent light,
talk to crazy Harry, count the change,
listen to top-forty radio. Mostly, I was alone.

Every stranger's suspect when you're alone.
A woman was beaten badly early one morning
by a man who sneaked in the back while she made
                                      change,
so I'd rehearse scenarios of scooping grease,
flinging it at the assailant's face, cooking the light
or dark flesh to curl away at the impact, angry pink.

The cab drivers came in every night, faces polished
                                      pink
and boyish, arriving in pairs or alone.
Their cabs clotted like moths at the building's light.
They were outlaws and brothers, despised men who
                                      rise in the morning.
They'd swagger, still dapper, if fattened on sweets
                                      and grease,
call me sugar and honey. I smiled. I kept the change.

Often I was too busy to see the darkness change,
flush from black to blue to early pink.
At four o'clock, my face smeared with congealed grease,
I think I was happiest, although most alone.
The harder hours were those of fullblown morning,
fighting depression, sleeping alone in the light.

Linda came in at six, awash with light,
businesslike, making sure there'd be enough change
to get her through the rigors of the morning.
She had a hundred uniforms; I remember pink.
Sometimes she'd cheat, leave me to work alone,
sneak out to flirt in parked cars, fleeing lifetimes
                              of grease.

I can see her cranking the hopper, measuring grease,
indefatigable, wired on coffee, just stopping to
                              light
her cigarettes. She didn't want to be alone.
It was only my fantasy that she could change,
stop wearing that silly, becoming pink,
burn free of the accidents, husband and children,
                              some morning.

I remember walking home those mornings, smelling
                              of grease,
amazed in summer's most delicate pink early light,
to shower, change, and sleep out the hot day alone.

tantrum

she hollers rage, denial,
who she is.
it is a nightmare,
children in the park.
her wrist's too small,
too fragile in your hand,
your anger's like a power
tool with teeth,
the concrete smoulders.

this is the fulcrum, edge.
the others stare
up with their anxious eyes,
diplomacy, knowing
they're little, knowing
you're adult

and history repeats.
you take the path,
you turn and drag her
screaming she was forced,
past all the swings and fathers,
out of the garden,
onto the pavement
rancid with august heat.

children

1.

what have you to fear?

it is not
extremes

the women
who can't stop
swelling
pushing strollers
feeling up fruit
in the market
hefting cabbage

the hot days hanging
off fire escapes
"psychic reader advisor"
in windows
ailanthus
plastic

it is not
these things

you left, leaving
flight plans, suicide
notes, plants
withered in the heat
of the locked
apartment, cats
damned to the hell
of the winter alley

and always
came back

you have no child
but the habit
of generations

mother croons
"deep purple"

and grandma
in a nightgown
combs her hair
wire pins on the table
her basement damp
in summer

you have this stock
of heirlooms, surfaces.
of breakfast, dinner
and authority, meat
rotting in the freezer
you can't throw out.

you have this childhood
smoother than
a lie. this fear
of children.

2.

your problem is
these legends of
frontier women

who yoked themselves
to the plough
when the horses dropped

who stooped in sweatshops
throughout the great depression
in minneapolis, omaha
and detroit, believed
in the god of pain
and repetition, the feeding
of children, the fucking
in the dark

3.

this child hurts you
like another self

an embryo sister curled
usurping the womb

your own well-
founded suspicions
look out
of her eyes

of the twentieth
century city, the
overcast skies
nursing grudges, missiles
and rain

beneath your roof
like the poor she is
always with you
like something you did
wrong or forgot
to do

you will spend
your life raising
other people's children

4.

what you want is
to be home
in your early twenties
alone
with your loneliness
poverty and plants
slowly augmenting their foliage
on window ledges
of narrow white-walled rooms

you want to write poems
that do not mention children

5.

reluctance
early memories
stain your morning

you
were the baby
of the difficult
birth, the unusual
presentation

you're
the barren daughter
illegitimate mother
cassandra
of off-color prophecies
the lumpen poet

life is a taste
you never fully acquired

6.

we choose
the children
being from non-being

indentured to us
our reasons
they arrive
howling oral histories
of nothingness

we enlist their help
in our experiment
their features sharpen
they forget everything

we let them in
on all the dreadful secrets
pronounce them human
and turn them loose in the forest

this then is your crime:
that you have wanted a child

7.

the sky is blue
and heaped with breast-
soft clouds
the maples begin
to turn away from green
and it is already september

you understand
how much you needed summer
how much you want
the places you won't live in:

evergreen island
off the pacific coast
rough pebbled beach and
cold rain-laden air

knowing you'll go
way down to the dark
of the year
you yet choose winter
streets and intricate rooms

almost as though you belonged
here, in the nexus
of freedom and unfreedom

you sit with friends
discussing nuclear war
and the problems
of raising children

who also once were a child
and now are grown

stories

> *Say it. Say it.*
>
> *The universe is made of stories,*
> *not of atoms.*
>
> —Muriel Rukeyser, "The Speed of Darkness"

1.

i felt i never
really knew
my father

close-mouthed about
lutherans, sisters,
his mother's death

like him
you never tell me
half enough

you drop hints only
i glimpse you
nursing a daughter

at two a.m.
while cramming
for comprehensives

you hated
showing me
the wedding pictures

you think i'm greedy
i want to know
too much

consult the evidence
of the text
you say

2.

all whalebone
and stiff upper lips
in daguerreotypes

our grandmothers
never tell
they lie to us

our grandmothers lie
in rooms of their own
in the ground

their stories in them
trapped
between their teeth

3.

we live
beneath one roof
with our separate stories

yours, of the child
you had to choose
to have

mine, of the unborn
child i must
not want

we hold each other
weeping
for our stories

i am weeping
for your freedom.
for my daughter.

the kitchen window

1.

in Bohack
a woman my age,
kid in a stroller,
is buying mayonnaise
and chocolate bars

another woman,
maybe sixty,
talks and talks
as she waits
at an empty counter

"it's a secret.
no one's saying
a goddamned thing.
what's your number?
where can i go
to get some service?"

the checker
checks

2.

i don't know anything
about the pain

labor

years/afternoons
raising kids

old hits
on the radio
dishes, diapers, mopping

the trash-filled yard
beneath the kitchen window
where trees
are going to
get rich quick and
bloom

i can't guess
the checker's
peculiar weariness,
which muscle
aches the most
with all that standing

i read Tillie Olsen
on the thirties

over and over
i try to imagine
my mother

3.

you show me the ring,
the date incised in gold,
the curled-up snapshots,
clothes to be given away:
high heels in a closet,
garter belt in a drawer,

"transcendentalist periodicals,"
"shakespeare's morphology,"
your grad school papers

the child
now learning to read
came out of your body

4.

"when you and me and mommy
live together,"
Anna tells me, "you
can be the daddy,
because when you play house
you need a mommy
and a daddy."

5.

and what will we do
together
in this place
with its tile,
its aqua kitchen,
back yard
concreted over

the suburbs
yawn in my genes
like inherited cancer

i'm left
with a love for/
horror of
formica

6.

we pioneer
this life. like
pulling teeth.

weeks when
sleep recedes,
spring, everything
healing or green,

the river under
thirty feet of rock.

there's no
outwitting pain.

mother,
anaesthetized
when i was born,

was there something,
once, you
passionately wanted?

is that
the secret?

7.

Anna, fierce
in her will
to control the kittens:

i want them to eat
and
now i want them to sleep

my mother
holed up in her
crazy '50's faith

that raising children's
some sort of
sculptural art

a lifetime, whispering
white
is the color
of culture

*but weeds
split the pavement*

*the world
cannot be saved*

*the whites
will be driven
at last
from Africa*

8.

no words, you say

we slip
through the nets
of speech

mother, lover, friend

9.

rain on the roof
i stroke the shape of your head
the soft hair snags
it tears my cold-cracked fingers

beneath, the living roots

all night you hold me
on and on we fly
into the storm

10.

how is it possible

space
around a life

for poems
for cats
for children

Hiroshima
five years before my birth

i'm baking bread
it's twelve degrees outside

green plant on the washer
sun through the kitchen window

WOMAN'S WORK/ II

likeness

but with you, also, i would want it.
forget what you learned, the sums
of your arduous schooling.
that is all labor, making something,
the grass grow where it never grew before;
that is capitalism, industry, hard pleasure
consuming the planet,
prodigious and admirable work.

this is love in the mirror. the light
girdles the galaxies and falls right back.
the dark star, kleptomaniac, absorbs.
this is only the world's most natural act

and though i know your body by my own
i need to fit my disembodied hands
around the difficult answers of your bones
and want to float you always when i plunge
all the way down
to tongue you into darkly grieving waves,
not of the sea-kind, but more resonant ones.

see, i can swim, can dance, can mourn
can open   my book   my body
my eyes for you under water.

the transplant

the plants
reach out new hands
toward the light

the cats adjust
the landlord's
satisfied

it seems only i
wake daily
to discover

this un-
accustomed fact
of our joined lives

indelible as
a scar
a newborn baby

uneasily present
like a heart
or kidney

the body
has not yet
accepted

september again

fall
clarifies brooklyn
makes me happy all over

classical light
the church steeple sky
in the window

summer our spilt milk

smog all blown away

on sunday we lie in bed late
breasts cool as chilled pears
(you need the blanket now)
and tell this story:

*how we will have fires
and birthdays
and work*

and always be good to each other

december: two views

1.

we're ten days into
another garbage strike,
the loading docks
of midtown office
buildings overflowing,
the sidewalks piled
with plastic garbage bags

as lights come on
all over the west village
the couples gather
in intimate cafes
beyond the rain

CLUB MEDITERRANEE
buses advertise

far from the forests
the trees, stacked
wait for christmas

2.

all day dry snow
has been falling
on the shoppers,
the mothers
dragging children,
the thinning traffic

it blows these cold
streets lonesome
like some prairie town
in minnesota
in my mother's youth

and darkness
empties our city

the children sleep

we are alone
in your room
at the top of the house

you cover me
with all your tenderness

the snow is blunting
even the pointed steeple
as we unveil,
begin the ancient rite

words for this

1.

easier to hear
the anger easier
to tell the pain
easier to see
the city rough-
edged incomplete
in the light
of morning

than to find
the words for
this your face
new beneath the
startled crown
of hair cunt
furled there
still as folded
hands you wait
my mouth

i have wanted
to speak of
it our flesh
embedded in
prehistory how
you re-
call me hold
forbid me
nothing

as i grip
hard your
waist hips
wide in
heavy seas

you know
you change
me as we
work together

pleasure
we wanted
splits
me i
am born

2.

tangle of leaves
in the under-
growth. who
walks, stalks,
crawls there. fear
of memory. change.
fear of falling
the oldest. and
the hunger.
how, every-
woman, we
rise.

i cannot see. i
cannot see
myself. you
are what stays,
has substance.
you convince me.
i am the planet
eclipsed. in-
consequent mass. you
are the warmth
at the center. you
are the mirror.

3.

but also pain. un-
acceptable levels.
real.

the german doctor
insisting she
can't remember

and the resistance
fighter testifying
how, having run
out of gas
in the night
they threw
the children
alive
into the furnace

recalling,
thirty years later
in her sunny room
in paris
the shouts
of the condemned
before their mouths
were taped

"It is not of death
I am afraid,
but the moment
before death."

arbeit macht frei

in hell
what frees us
from the memory
of being held

4.

and in the end
do we want
what we say we
want. time,
our distracted
mother, grabs
our wrists
and hauls us,
howling, where
we would not go.
your phone
voice cool,
stretched
across several
states. it's you
i would shelter,
knowing we can-
not save
even the children,
even our own skins,
tomato vines
rotting beneath
november rain.

5.

you go
for the weekend,
leave me alone
in my life.
it's quiet here
when i control
the house.
i set the rooms
in order, hail
cats in
from the yard,

stripped, defence-
less, shocked
by an almost-
bare tree,
a child's chair
submerged in a
drift of leaves,
a winter sky gilt-
edged with
violent light.

Notes:

"It is not of death I am afraid, but the moment before death": This line is from the poem "Areas of Silence" by Susan Sherman.

Arbeit macht frei: "Work frees": slogan inscribed by the Nazis above the entrance to Dachau concentration camp.

impermanence

your face, these rooms, conspire, loved through use,
tempt me with dreams of easeful permanence.
no. i conspire, fabricate, adapt
my childhood fiction of the family, wrapped,
behemoth, mammoth, in suburban death.

see how we go about our busyness,
stolid, unconscious, bourgeois as the cats,
more self-important with our politics;
forge on through numbing haze of incident,
a smog of meetings, phonecalls, shit, shitwork;

rise bright and early, double-lock the door,
too-civilized sisters scared of what we glimpsed
while flying eyeless by the instruments
into the nature-crazed interior
where pleasure equals anarchy and death.

you fear, i fear extremes invite extremes;
the cunt splits open and the mirrors crack;
two worlds collide and somebody gets hurt;
our friction only hones a cutting edge.
best train for the lonely long run, practice death

and save up life for later, like dessert.
dear apparition, semi-solid sweet,
the rooms are rented, and the faces changed
decade to decade. nothing makes up for that,
for death, for life. i lie with you alone.

the trees: connecticut

1.

up for the weekend
i recall
early lessons

tree patterns
are etched behind
my oregon eyes

though this is
cezanne pine-
country, full of light

the birds at their singing
all the livelong day
beginning at four

here, history's
a pneumatic drill
in the city

indolent, displaced
i stretch
in the sun

the flesh moves
easy-muscled
through lakewater

i study
the tabula rasa
of teenage bodies

the curlered mothers
ten years
will turn them into

feed curses
and peanut butter
to pallid children

2.

it happened once when i was riding
in a car in western massachusetts. you
in the car ahead of me. your mouth moving
behind the glass making words in a
conversation i couldn't hear. you separate,
strange as a piece of my own body moving
detached and vulnerable over sharply-
curving roads. over dangerous space
untouchable now by me.

the delicate mechanism of brakes and steering.
the bridge that ices before the road.
the darkness coming on.

3.

she-goat tied
in the firefly-
starred field

moon full up
in cabin-dark
you wait

our bodies remember
return through time
to the clearing

the trees
witness
our meeting

your breasts
complete me.   anchor me
in this life.

FLYING OVER MY LIFE

dialectics

Outside and inside are just an illusion.

—Assata Shakur, "What Is Left?"

1.

scarlike, the continent
puckers, drawn together
by dreams, by what
i remember: the bulk
of land traversed
to get here, not
in airplanes, unreal,
but actually, on roads

and even winter wearies
and ice breaks up
on the river
piss-yellow sun
soaks through the haze
above Flatbush
cells poise to divide
the first forced crocuses
choke the florist's shop

too long i have been
floating, dreaming
mountains, the future
safe like money
in the bank, a lack
of limits, fistful
of lottery tickets
dreaming (what's wrong
with this picture?)
i am the exception

you can be anything
is what they taught me
down the road apiece
i caught them in their lie
i have known the odd half-life
of the emigree
wintering on the fat
of the old regime
scraping the privilege, bitter
from my plate

i'm what
i have
to hate
white skin
and history

2. (Assata on trial in New Jersey)

contradictions, ice cream
at the demo, a beautiful
day in New Brunswick,
picket fences, black cops,
neat red brick jail, that
all-white jury

we shout around the courthouse
free to leave
to take the bus
be someone else in the city

and never yet for us
the patient faces
that watch the prosecutor
know they can do this

and never the handcuffs
and never the sun denied
and never the muscles destroyed
and never the love postponed
and never the life abridged
and never the isolation
articulated in concrete
and never the testing
never the testing of limits
and never New Jersey's
obliterating eyes

and never anything irrevocable

and never the headlines:
CHESIMARD GUILTY OF MURDER

3. (the road)

spring comes late to these
upthrust slabs
of granite
evergreens sheltering
rotten snow

maples bud red
in the hollows
it is raining
onto rock, onto elms
knee-deep
in watery fields,
onto bright bulldozed
embankments, barns
falling in

to see clearly, is that
the greatest gift?

this austere country
floods me with its
narrow band of colors:
dark-layered earth
dark sky

brimming
i drive
north

4.

in childbirth
you focus on technique

how difficult
to stay awake
keep moving

like climbing Everest
without equipment
snowblind
hand over hand
up the ice face

how difficult
to live inside my story

5. (reading Plath's *Letters Home;*
    rereading *Ariel*)

i skim like a thriller
these last communiques.
the hyperactive poet
proclaims she's coping.
"I'm happier than ever."
manic. dead-ended.

and yet the release it is,
the icy comfort
after the cloying tone
of Ted and babies.
"I am a genius poet."
she knew her power,
knew images pouring,
the epileptic's aura.
hoped, for a moment,
that gift could be turned
to profit. but signed
her suicide, her QED.

nothing
is preparation
for these poems,
the mathematics,
cold unanswerable facts,
pain buffed
to the luster
of science,
impersonal art.
i will not deny
her February death.
i tell you this,
who have no use
for quitters:

the blood
jet is
self-
hatred

6. (upstate poetry tour)

i ask what lake this is.
they tell me Erie.
there are widows' walks here,
nowhere near the sea.
there's pinball
to be played
in the Greyhound station
in Rochester, ugly
under April rain

i want to talk
about these pitted
faces. the station
is the same
as any other:
mixture of sweat,
impatience, lack
of sleep. someone
with choices
would not choose
to sit here.

the word "workingclass"
doesn't say it
doesn't describe

on the bus, a woman
holding her year-old baby
six or eight hours,
rocked and cursed to sleep

how the houses
left unpainted
go downhill faster

or the snatched, furtive
pleasures, leaching
away of a life.

7.

snow in a strange city
hungry in the morning
in a cluttered room
that makes me think of Portland
i pick the book from the shelf
and read before breakfast
of the Cuban woman
who told the prison guards
If he has not talked under torture
much less will I
when they brought her
the bloody eye
of her blinded brother.
of several women
who had been prostitutes.
of one who died
disarming a faulty bomb.
of Che not come back
from the hills. of anonymous
others.

it says here
certain scars
can never heal.

8.

i am a lesbian, forfeit
the universal. i cannot
tour Cuba in comfort
nor read my poetry
to rooms with kind men in them
smiling kindly
to halls with well-
heeled poetry
lovers in them
clamoring for the truth.

9.

listen, my ancestors
rooted up stumps
from their thin-soiled farms
in northern Minnesota,
ate roots
before the first greens
could be gathered.
they knew
an immediacy of fields,
the next row of corn
to be planted.

10.

to choose a side
is only the half of it
and nothing is simple
and nothing is finished, ever
the truth is dense and shaded,
a living forest
there are no guarantees

to choose reality
is to wake in chains
on stony ground
in the ice-edged desert dawn

all things sharp-outlined
peculiarly themselves

it is to begin

flying over my life

*over and over
the plane
heaves
gigantic
onto the runway
dragging
its hulking
shadow*

*over and
over
and we
alive
within
watching*

1.

how i love to look out on
these flat December mornings

mornings
when the boiler isn't broken
and heat comes knocking up

the pigeons know to turn together
now black now silver
in the sun

the smoke lifts coldly

it is winter-dry
the rings
slide loose on my fingers

all the doors shut

2.

it is fire-season, morgue-
season, it is the bottom line

arriving home
to firetrucks in the street

some junkie played with matches
in the hall

which looks like Dresden
nineteen-forty-five

and there is falling plaster
there is a leaky faucet
there is a window sash
too rotten to be hammered

the old wood doors from the '90's
have been replaced with metal

3.

i am a woman.
i hurry through my life
phoning, spraying for roaches,
signing petitions

i type
i do dishes
i mind children

often i am too tired
to get it right

4.

and Capital rides through the streets
handsome and insane
a syphilitic
still able to fuck his wife

and Capital runs
amok in the streets,
psycho, mad dog, won't
somebody hurry, shoot him

*hush, don't say that
on the telephone*

5.

running through the park:
it's about control of pain

on the softball diamond
the only thing not frozen
is the wasted arc
that leaps from the drinking fountain
sheeting the field in ice

Black woman walks her child
in windless silence

the Anglo-Saxons sleep
on the grave-
hived hill

the cop car waits for no good
by the lake

6. (Airport '77)

it's mechanics and demographics
that kill me
not planes

pale faces, doors
that open of themselves
the ads for Forbes and Fortune
standup bars

and here's the wrung-out
replica of ads
in navy stretch pants
chewing gum all day
punching numbers
into that computer

7.

Buffalo frozen
in a cube of smog
cloverleaves
we rise above

thinking of Robert Frost
his arrogant poem
read out for the cameras
in winter Washington
before i understood,
could understand

the land was ours
before we were the land's

this bruised earth
corseted
redundant roads

up here in the sun
the man slumped next to me
in a corduroy jacket
reading Businessweek

could be my father

8.

traveling always in
that limbo of the
airport
corridor
dream

Buffalo
the steel mills
and cemeteries
poking through dirty snow
where people live
in real houses

a child in a kitchen
in feeted pink pajamas
oven-warmed
eating her rice krispies

the buildings poor and close
with strips of yard

over and over
the lives i could have lived

9.

the land
was never ours
we were never
the land's

set it to music
sing it if you can

recite it for state occasions
poetfathers

slaveships
and smallpox
smuggled in ratty blankets

how the ghettos, projects
shift on the face
of cities
the tenements fall
and Pharaoh builds them again

tell us
the one about progress

you never step
in the same cash nexus
twice

10.

we have forgotten
the other extremes of August

it is winter
with winter's
peculiar hardships

the winos are wiping windshields
at stoplights
on Houston Street and Bowery

it will be Christmas

the clockwork dolls
will be asked for,
wrapped, unwrapped,
admired, wound, broken,
slapped
for their stupid pains,
their fifteen-second trick.

11.

and we are a shadow
tracking
streets and houses
a mote in the eye
of suns
spotting lives
and lifetimes
under us
as we drop
mortal
straight to the world

12.

this happened
before you were born

this happens

in the great room
warmlit
the mothers
give their children suck
carry them
up to bed

we who are born and die
on these long marches

fill rented rooms
with shabby human things
call it a life

this is a life

Note:

"The land was ours before we were the land's":
This line is from Robert Frost's "The Gift
Outright," read at John F. Kennedy's inaugural
in 1960.

Additional copies of **Waking at the Bottom of the Dark** may be ordered from:

**Long Haul Press
P.O. Box 592
Van Brunt Station
Brooklyn, NY 11215**

Enclose $3.00 plus $.50 postage/handling per copy. New York City residents add 8% sales tax. New York State residents add 4% sales tax. Make checks payable to Long Haul Press.

Jan Clausen's **After Touch** (poems, 1975) may also be ordered from Long Haul Press. Enclose $2.00 plus $.50 postage/handling plus sales tax where applicable.

40% trade discount on bookstore orders.